YOUR PASSPORT TO
SAUDI ARABIA

by Golriz Golkar

CAPSTONE PRESS
a capstone imprint

Published by Capstone Press, an imprint of Capstone
1710 Roe Crest Drive, North Mankato, Minnesota 56003
capstonepub.com

Library of Congress Cataloging-in-Publication Data is available on the Library
of Congress website.
ISBN: 9781669058625 (hardcover)
ISBN: 9781669058571 (paperback)
ISBN: 9781669058588 (ebook PDF)

Summary: What is it like to live in or visit Saudi Arabia? What makes Saudi
Arabia's culture unique? Explore the geography, traditions, and daily lives of
Saudi Arabian people.

Editorial Credits
Editor: Carrie Sheely; Designer: Bobbie Nuytten; Media Researcher: Rebekah
Hubstenberger; Production Specialist: Whitney Schaefer

Image Credits
Alamy: CPA Media Pte Ltd, 9; Associated Press: Saudi Information Ministry, 21;
Capstone Press: Eric Gohl, 5; Getty Images: Clive Brunskill, 27, Evans/Three
Lions, 13, General Photographic Agency, 12, iStock/Aviator70, 25, iStock/
JohnnyGreig, 18, iStock/mtcurado, 11, Jordan Pix, 14, Manuel Queimadelos/
Quality Sport Images, 28, Mint Images, 17, xavierarnau, 29, adznano3, Cover,
Alexander Ingerman, 19, BY-_-BY, 22, memomemory, 6

Design Elements
Getty Images: iStock/Yevhenii Dubinko; Shutterstock: Flipser, Gil C (flag), Net
Vector, pingebat, twenty1studio, (map)

Printed and bound in China. PO 5593

CONTENTS

Words in **bold** are in the glossary.

CHAPTER ONE

WELCOME TO SAUDI ARABIA!

The sun rises over the Ṭuwayq Mountains. At the end of the mountain range, rocky cliffs soar above a glistening desert. They offer a sweeping view of a landscape where trade **caravans** traveled long ago. These cliffs are Jebel Fihrayn. They stand tall in Saudi Arabia, a modern country with an ancient past.

A DESERT LAND

Saudi Arabia is located in western Asia. It makes up most of the Arabian Peninsula. Saudi Arabia is bordered by Kuwait, Jordan, and Iraq to the north. Yemen borders the country to the south. The Red Sea lies to the west. Qatar, Oman, the United Arab Emirates, and the Persian Gulf lie to the east.

FACT

Jebel Fihrayn is also known as the Edge of the World.

MAP OF SAUDI ARABIA

N
W E
S

■ Capital City
● City
▲ Landmark
■ Asir National Park

SAUDI ARABIA

Dammam

RIYADH
Medina
● Prophet's Mosque
Kingdom Centre Tower

Jeddah
▲ King Fahd's Fountain

Asir National Park

Farasan Island
Jazan

Explore Saudi Arabia's cities and landmarks.

In the north, Saudi Arabia is mostly desert with valleys. A rocky **plateau** makes up the central region. The southwest is mountainous. Sandy beaches are found on the east and west coasts.

The climate of Saudi Arabia is dry. Winters are cool, and summers are hot. The southwestern coast has **monsoons** with large amounts of rainfall.

5

SAUDI PEOPLE

More than 30 million people live in Saudi Arabia. Most Saudis live in cities. A small number live in rural areas. Almost every Saudi has Arab **ethnicity**. They are descendants of **nomadic** tribes of the Arabian Peninsula. Most Saudis are native to the country. Other people came from different countries on the Arabian Peninsula. Some Saudis have African and Asian backgrounds. Nearly all Saudis are Muslims. They follow the religion of Islam. Islam is the official religion in the country.

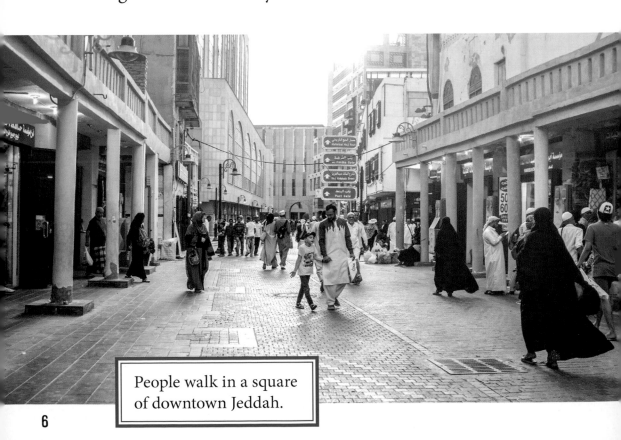

People walk in a square of downtown Jeddah.

FACT FILE

OFFICIAL NAME: .... KINGDOM OF SAUDI ARABIA
POPULATION: 32,375,000
LAND AREA: .... 829,996 SQ. MI. (2,149,690 SQ KM)
CAPITAL: .... RIYADH
MONEY: .... SAUDI RIYAL
GOVERNMENT: .... ABSOLUTE MONARCHY
LANGUAGE: .... ARABIC
GEOGRAPHY: Saudi Arabia is located in western Asia on the Arabian Peninsula. It borders Kuwait, Jordan, and Iraq to the north, Yemen to the south, and the Red Sea to the west. Qatar, Oman, the United Arab Emirates, and the Persian Gulf are to the east.
NATURAL RESOURCES: Saudi Arabia has petroleum, iron ore, gold, and copper.

Arabic is the official language of Saudi Arabia. People also speak English.

Saudis have an old and rich **culture**. They are famous for their music, literature, arts, and architecture.

CHAPTER TWO

HISTORY OF SAUDI ARABIA

People arrived on the Arabian Peninsula around 8000 BCE. They hunted and gathered food.

Starting around 6000 BCE, the first settlements appeared. By the 100s CE, settlers were living in hundreds of tribes and kingdoms across the peninsula.

By the 800s CE, the Arabian Peninsula was a major trade center. Caravans crossed the region. They carried goods to countries across the continent. Goods included dates, spices, silk, and precious stones.

THE ROOTS OF THE ISLAMIC EMPIRE

Around 610 CE, the Prophet Muhammad established Islam. He led his followers to Medina and Mecca. He started the Islamic Empire. Within 100 years, the Islamic Empire stretched from Spain to parts of India and China. Many Muslims began visiting the peninsula. They traveled to Medina and Mecca to pray.

Traders in caravans often rode camels as they crossed the Arabian Peninsula.

Arabic became an important international language. The Arabian Peninsula turned into a learning hub. This Golden Age of Islam lasted from the 700s to the 1500s. Muslim **scholars** contributed to science, literature, and art.

In 1517, the Ottoman Empire took over the Arabian Peninsula. However, Saudi ruling families held most of the power during Ottoman rule. By the 1600s, the Islamic Empire had broken up. Smaller Muslim kingdoms formed.

In 1727, a local ruler, Muhammad bin Saud, joined forces with Muslim scholar Muhammad bin Abdul Wahhab. They created the first Saudi state. By the early 1800s, the Saudi state ruled most of the Arabian Peninsula.

Officials of the first Saudi state gathered at Salwa Palace in Al-Dir'iyyah. Today, the palace is restored.

Throughout the 1800s, Saudi rulers fought many battles. Ottomans, Egyptians, and Arabian families wanted power. At times, Saudi power was lost. In 1891, the Al-Rashid **Dynasty** of the Arabian Peninsula took over the Saudi state.

MODERN SAUDI ARABIA

In 1902, Ibn Saud, the son of the last Saudi ruler, decided to take back power. He marched into Riyadh with a group of followers. They stormed the city's military base, the Masmak Fortress.

Ibn Saud's group overthrew the Al-Rashid family. Over the next 30 years, Ibn Saud claimed back more Saudi territories. In 1932, the Najd and Hijaz regions were unified. They became the Kingdom of Saudi Arabia. King Ibn Saud ruled the new Islamic state.

Ibn Saud

Workers lay an oil pipeline in the desert of Saudi Arabia in the mid-1950s.

King Ibn Saud improved communication systems and roads. More people began farming. In 1938, oil was discovered in Saudi Arabia. Saudis sold oil to the United States and other countries. Saudi Arabia became wealthy. In 1953, King Ibn Saud died. His son, Crown Prince Saud, became king. To this day, Saudi Arabia is ruled by direct male **heirs** of King Ibn Saud.

When King Fahd died in 2005, his half-brother Abdullah became king. He helped improve women's rights. He announced that women could vote in **municipal** elections and run for government office starting in 2015. He also made government changes. In 2015, King Salman became the ruler of the country.

Saudi women cast their votes for municipal elections at a polling station in 2015.

TIMELINE OF SAUDI HISTORY

ABOUT 610 CE: Prophet Muhammad establishes Islam.

1517: The Ottoman Empire takes over the Arabian Peninsula.

1600s: The Islamic Empire breaks into smaller Muslim kingdoms.

1727: The first Saudi state forms.

1891: The Al-Rashid family takes over the Saudi state.

1902: Ibn Saud storms Masmak Fortress and takes back the Saudi state.

1932: The Kingdom of Saudi Arabia forms.

1938: Workers discover oil in Saudi Arabia.

1953: Ibn Saud dies, and Crown Prince Saud becomes king.

2015: King Abdullah dies, and King Salman takes the throne.

2018: A ban on women's driving is lifted.

2019: Saudi Arabia officially opens to non-Muslim tourists.

SAUDI TRIBES

Before King Ibn Saud formed the modern country, the tribes followed their own rules. They often fought with one another. The king needed to grow his power. He made a list of common Islamic teachings that the tribes accepted. He encouraged tribal members and his own children to marry outside their tribes. Today, many tribal members are linked to the Saudi ruling family through marriage.

CHAPTER THREE

EXPLORE SAUDI ARABIA

Saudi Arabia has many ancient sites, natural areas, and landmarks that people enjoy visiting.

Beaches are very popular. Visitors swim in the turquoise waters off Half Moon Bay Beach. Umluj Beach is a good spot for watching birds. Diving is a popular sport off Farasan Al Kabir Beach.

ANCIENT SITES

Hegra is located in the northern Medina Province. Arab **merchants** called Nabataeans built the city. Visitors can see large, decorated tombs with engravings and cave drawings. They date back to the 100s BCE. The tombs house the bodies of Nabataean families and high-ranking officials.

The Nabataean cave tombs in Hegra have carved designs on their fronts.

Jubbah is located in the Nafud Desert. Visitors can see desert rock engravings. There are engravings of different animals. They date back to the 5500s BCE.

The Jawatha **Mosque** is in Al-Kilabiyah. It is considered the oldest mosque in the eastern Arabian Peninsula. It was built 1,400 years ago during Prophet Muhammad's lifetime.

EXCITING CITIES

Riyadh is a modern city. At the National Museum, visitors can learn about Saudi history. The Kingdom Centre is one of the tallest skyscrapers in the country. It offers a city view from its sky bridge.

Jazan is a port city located on Saudi Arabia's Red Sea coast. Visitors enjoy boat rides, fishing trips, and diving.

Dammam is the capital of the Eastern Province. The city has sandy beaches, outdoor markets, and street music.

The Kingdom Centre rises to a height of 992 feet (302 meters).

Jeddah is a waterfront city on the Red Sea. Visitors can see the Al Rahma Mosque built over the water. The city's King Fahd's Fountain is the tallest in the world. It shoots water more than 800 feet (244 m) in the air!

ANIMALS

The Riyadh National Zoo is home to more than 1,000 animals. The rare African houbara bustard bird can be found there.

Saudi Arabia also has protected parks. Asir National Park is home to native plants and animals such as the Nubian ibex.

Nubian ibex live in mountainous desert areas.

CHAPTER FOUR

DAILY LIFE

Most Saudis live in cities. They live in apartments or houses. Many **generations** of the same family may share a home. People in cities get around by car or bus. Many work in service jobs, sales, or tourism.

People who live in rural areas may live in mudbrick houses. They often work on date or wheat farms. Some work on groundwater drilling sites.

DRILLING FOR WATER

Saudi Arabia has no lakes or rivers and receives little rain. Underground water sources called aquifers are an important water source. These aquifers formed millions of years ago. Through drilling wells, the Saudi government has accessed enough water for both home and farm use.

TRADITIONS AND FAMILY

Some Saudi men wear traditional clothes. They include a headdress and a long robe worn over pants. Until 2018, women had to wear a headscarf, or hijab, and a black cloak called an abaya in public. The rules have been relaxed. Today, women must cover their bodies but do not have to dress traditionally.

Other rules have eased as well. In 2018, women were allowed to drive after a long ban. In 2019, women over 21 years old were given the right to travel abroad without approval from a male guardian. Laws separating men and women in public have also been relaxed.

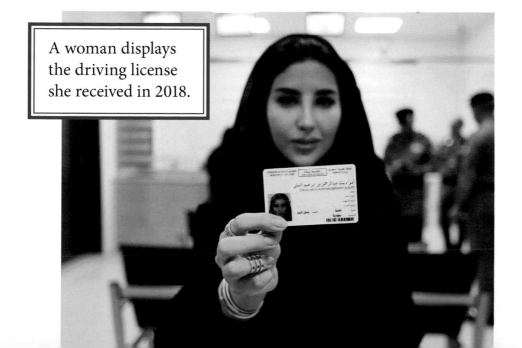

A woman displays the driving license she received in 2018.

FLAVORFUL FOOD

Saudis enjoy many flavorful dishes. The national dish is *kabsa*. It is a meat dish cooked with rice. *Tharid* is a spicy lamb stew served with flatbread. *Gursan* is a meat soup cooked with vegetables and bread pieces. Saudis also enjoy shawarma, which is roasted meat served with pita bread. It is a popular street food.

Saudis enjoy dates, fresh fruit, and pudding for dessert. People eat date or nut cookies called maamoul on holidays.

shawarma

MAAMOUL

These cookies are enjoyed on religious holidays. You will need an adult to help you make them.

Ingredients:
- ½ cup butter
- ¼ cup olive oil
- 2 tablespoons sugar
- 2 ½ cups all-purpose flour
- 2 tablespoons rose water
- 3 tablespoons milk
- 2/3 lb. Medjool dates, pitted and chopped
- powdered sugar for dusting

Directions:
1. Preheat the oven to 350°F.
2. In a small saucepan, melt the butter over medium heat. Mix in the oil and sugar.
3. Pour the butter mixture into a large bowl. Add the flour and mix the ingredients together by hand to make a dough.
4. Add the rose water. Then add the milk, one tablespoon at a time. Keep kneading the dough by hand.
5. Set aside the dough for 30 minutes. Then divide the dough into about 30 small balls.
6. Ask an adult to help you blend the chopped dates in a food processor. Make 30 small date balls.
7. Take a dough ball and flatten it. Place a date ball in the middle. Bring together the dough edges to seal the cookie shut. Gently flatten the cookie by hand.
8. Repeat for the remaining dough and date balls.
9. Place the cookies on a baking sheet and bake for 15 to 20 minutes until light brown.
10. Remove the cookies from the oven and let them cool. Sprinkle them with powdered sugar and serve.

CHAPTER FIVE
HOLIDAYS AND CELEBRATIONS

On September 23, Saudis celebrate Saudi National Day. It is the day the country was founded in 1932. Parades, fireworks, music, and food mark the holiday. Saudis dress in green and white. These are the colors of their flag.

HONORING ISLAM

Mecca and Medina are still the holiest cities in Islam today. Saudis and Muslims from other countries make **pilgrimages** there. Medina is the city where the Prophet Muhammad lived and died. Muslims visit his tomb at the Prophet's Mosque.

Mecca is where the Prophet Muhammad was born. Every year, more than 2 million Muslims from around the world go there for the hajj, or pilgrimage. For five days, Muslims pray and participate in rituals.

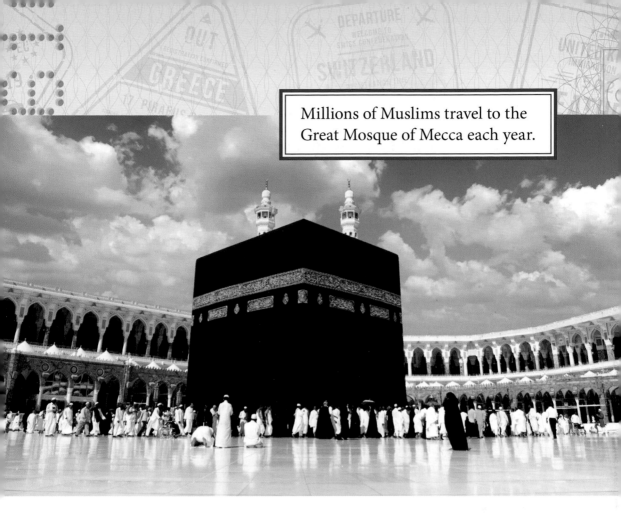

Millions of Muslims travel to the Great Mosque of Mecca each year.

At the end of the hajj, Muslims all over the world celebrate Eid al-Adha. Saudis spend time with friends and family. They attend prayer services.

Saudis **fast** during the holy month of Ramadan. They do not eat from sunrise until sunset. They pray many times a day. At the end of Ramadan, they celebrate Eid al-Fitr. This holiday ends the fast. Muslims pray. They visit relatives and share meals. Children receive gifts.

CHAPTER SIX

SPORTS AND RECREATION

Saudis enjoy many sports. Traditional sports include camel racing. Several cities host camel races. Winners receive cash prizes. Horse racing is also popular. Jockeys from all over the world race in events. The yearly Saudi Cup offers the world's biggest cash prize for horse racing. In 2023, the winner took home a $10 million prize.

Soccer is another favorite sport. Saudis watch local teams compete in the King's Cup. They also cheer on their national team at the World Cup.

FACT

In 2023, the women's national soccer team won its first international tournament.

Salem Al-Dawsari (left) of the Saudi Arabia men's national team celebrates after scoring a goal in a 2022 World Cup match.

Women compete in a beach soccer match at the NEOM Beach Games in 2022.

Saudis also enjoy golf. Professional golf championships are held for both men and women.

Water sports are also popular. They include sailing, kiteboarding, and windsurfing. In 2022, the NEOM Beach Games were held in Saudi Arabia. They included events in kitesurfing, triathlon, basketball, and other sports. More than 500 athletes from 25 countries competed.

THE HUNTER

The Hunter is a Saudi game that combines freeze tag and hide and seek. You will need at least three players. It can be played indoors or outdoors.

1. One player is chosen as the hunter.
2. As the hunter counts to 50, the other players hide.
3. When the hunter reaches 50, they must search for the other players.
4. When a player is found, the hunter tags them. The player must remain in place until the hunter finds all the players.
5. When all the players have been found, the first person found becomes the new hunter. The game begins again with the new hunter.

Saudi Arabia is a country of both old and new. It blends beautiful landscapes with bustling modern cities. People enjoy its striking buildings, beaches, and other attractions.

In northwestern Saudi Arabia, a natural formation called Elephant Rock stands 170 feet (52 m) tall.

GLOSSARY

caravan (KA-ruh-van)
a group of travelers on a journey

culture (KUHL-chuhr)
a people's way of life, ideas, art, customs, and traditions

dynasty (DYE-nuh-stee)
a series of rulers belonging to the same family

ethnicity (eth-NI-suh-tee)
a group of people who share the same background

fast (FAST)
to give up eating for a period of time

generation (jen-uh-RAY-shuhn)
a group of people born around the same time

heir (AIR)
someone who has been or will be left a title, property, or money

merchant (MUR-chuhnt)
a person who buys and sells goods

monsoon (mon-SOON)
a weather season that has very heavy rainfall

mosque (MOSK)
a building used by Muslims for worship

municipal (myu-NI-suh-pul)
related to a primarily urban political unit

nomadic (no-MAD-ik)
traveling from place to place instead of living in one spot

pilgrimage (PIL-gruhm-uhj)
a journey to a holy place for religious reasons

plateau (plah-TOW)
an area of high, flat land

scholar (SKOL-ur)
a person who has done advanced study in a special field

READ MORE

Hamby, Rachel. *Ramadan*. Minneapolis: Pop!, 2021.

Orr, Tamra B. *Saudi Arabian Heritage*. Ann Arbor, MI: Cherry Lake Publishing, 2019.

Spanier, Kristine. *Saudi Arabia*. Minneapolis: Pogo Books, 2021.

INTERNET SITES

Easy Science for Kids: Saudi Arabia
easyscienceforkids.com/all-about-saudi-arabia

DK Findout!: Eid
dkfindout.com/us/more-find-out/festivals-and-holidays/eid/

Kiddle: Islamic Golden Age Facts for Kids
kids.kiddle.co/Islamic_Golden_Age

INDEX

ABOUT THE AUTHOR

Golriz Golkar is the author of more than 70 books for children. Inspired by her work as an elementary school teacher, she loves to write the kinds of books that children are excited to read. Golriz holds a B.A. in American literature and culture from UCLA and a master's degree in education from the Harvard Graduate School of Education. Golriz lives in France with her husband and young daughter, and they all love reading together.

SELECT BOOKS IN THIS SERIES

YOUR PASSPORT TO AUSTRALIA
YOUR PASSPORT TO BRAZIL
YOUR PASSPORT TO CUBA
YOUR PASSPORT TO EGYPT
YOUR PASSPORT TO ENGLAND
YOUR PASSPORT TO GERMANY
YOUR PASSPORT TO JAPAN
YOUR PASSPORT TO MEXICO
YOUR PASSPORT TO PORTUGAL
YOUR PASSPORT TO SAUDI ARABIA